Bright ideas
for Early Years

Learning Through Play

Janet Morris & Linda Mort

Published by Scholastic Publications Ltd,
Villiers House, Clarendon Avenue,
Leamington Spa, Warwickshire CV32 5PR.

© 1990 Scholastic Publications Ltd

Reprinted 1991, 1993

Written by Linda Mort and Janet Morris
Edited by Christine Lee
Sub-edited by Anne Faundez
Designed by Sue Limb
Illustrations by Jane Andrews
Photographs by:
Tom Blau page 37
Stan Gamester page 63
John Harris pages 51 and 91
Keith Hawkins pages 21 and 77
Chris Kelly page 9
Adrian Rowland page 5
Cover by Martin Chillmaid

Artwork by Liz Preece,
Castle Graphics, Kenilworth
Printed in Great Britain by
Loxley Brothers Ltd, Sheffield

British Library Cataloguing in Publication Data
Mort, Linda
    Bright ideas for early years.
    Learning through play.
    1. Nursery schools. Teaching
    I. Title II. Morris, Janet
    372.1102

    ISBN 0-590-76332-6

Contents

Acknowledgements

We should like to acknowledge our use of some of the ideas in the following articles:

- 'Up, down and round', by Cathy Nutbrown. Article on schemas, in *Child Education*, May 1989.

See 'Swings and roundabouts', page 18.

- 'Investigative Play', by Lynne Bartholomew. Section on 'Making parcels', in *Child Education*, May 1989.

See 'It's nearly Christmas', page 29.

- 'Puppet Play', by June Hurst. Article on making puppets, in *Child Education*, July 1986.

See 'Puppet show', page 86.

We have made a brief reference to:

Young Children Learning by Professor B Tizard and M Hughes (Fontana 1984).

Introduction

An early years' curriculum should provide children with opportunities for:

- Research of their own world, through firsthand experiences, using the body and all the senses;
- Reflection on these experiences, through conversation with adults and other children;
- Re-creation of these experiences, through representation in a wide variety of forms.

A child's research of her world must be based on her own choice. An early years' curriculum should be centred on individuals and founded on personal interests and motivations. In order to achieve this, staff must create close links with a child's home environment and carefully observe children in order to see the world, as far as possible, from the 'child's-eye view'. An adult can never, of course, totally share a child's vision, but there are various 'clues' which can help adults gain an insight into the child's world.

Staff can learn much about children's predominant interests and conceptual development by close observation of their spontaneous physical play, for example, recurrent physical movements, as they try to give physical embodiment to abstract concepts they are trying to assimilate.

Early years' teachers should encourage children to bring in toys and other personal possessions as they can give a valuable insight into what motivates a child and provide a starting point for conversation. Similarly, discussions about a child's drawings, paintings and models can reveal much about how a child is relating to the world.

A further clue can be provided by 'committed listening' on the part of the staff to what children are really saying. Teachers should give children time to explore concepts orally and should not be in a hurry to conclude a conversation by making a quick 'teaching' point. This may be at odds with, or irrelevant to, what the child is really trying to understand and express.

This kind of genuine listening is easier for staff to do if they ask the children as many authentic questions as possible — questions to which they, the staff, do not know the answers in advance. For example, a staff member could ask a child to describe the personality of her pet kitten. This kind of question is different from the 'closed' question, to which the teacher already knows the answer, and which does not encourage extended conversations. A closed question is limiting and offers no opportunities for an adult to find out more about a child.

Research such as that by Professor B Tizard and M Hughes in *Young Children Learning* (Fontana 1984) has shown that reflection on the part of a young child can best be encouraged through relaxed conversations, especially in the home. It is helpful if teachers can gain an insight into these important home experiences. This same body of research has also examined the nature of children's questioning at school and in the home. It has been found that many children who are intellectually curious and forever asking questions at home do not do so at school. It is thought that the traditional use of adults' closed questions can put some children into a passive, answering role which can be difficult to break. Again, a change of emphasis from the traditional type of questioning to more relaxed dialogues can be valuable.

Intellectual thinking can be developed by school staff answering the children's questions, and casually pointing out phenomena which may be of interest to children. This can help to ensure that children maintain their ever-curious, questioning, active thinking both at home and at school.

The re-creation of children's experiences at home and at school is essential for synthesising all aspects of development — social, emotional, physical and intellectual. Careful provision by staff can enable children's re-creation to be broad and to take many forms — oral, physical, imaginative and aesthetic. The early years' curriculum should be based on children's needs for space, experiential learning, time for concentration, choice, informal conversation and purposeful play.

Through careful observation and record-keeping, there can be a natural continuum between the child-centred early years' curriculum, based on developmental needs, and the National Curriculum. The subject-based programmes of study of the National Curriculum should not, and need not be imposed on young children in 'out-of-context' direct teaching.

Successful learning in the National Curriculum depends on active thinking and communication skills. These cannot be taught directly, but must be nurtured from the beginning by teachers sensitive to children's interests and needs.

It is important that staff capture children's imaginations and enthusiasm for learning by having knowledge of their interests, and the expertise to develop these. The ideas in this book are all based on experience of three- to six-year-olds' most popular interests and pursuits. Many of the ideas begin with an example of a child's comment, frequently heard at (pre) school. Each idea offers one or more 'next steps' to develop the child's initial interest through a variety of experiences which share common elements. In this way, a child is helped to develop concepts, and he is enabled to follow his particular 'learning thread'. These 'threads' help to open up his initial interest.

En route, many mathematical, scientific and language concepts may be developed, as teachers offer the child opportunities to research, reflect on and re-create experiences which are based on, but not restricted to, his personal view of the world.

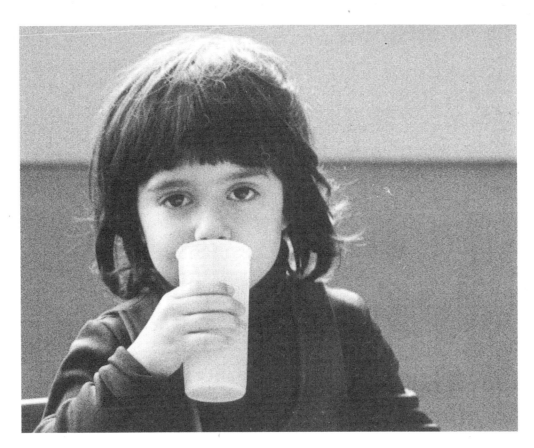

Just me

Chapter one

Young children have an egocentric perception of the world based largely on their senses. This can often have an overwhelming effect on their emotions. For example, a child who is thirsty cannot function properly until he has had a drink.

This chapter offers suggestions to help teachers recognise the importance of these sensations, and to use them to help children express themselves and come to terms with their feelings.

Physical movement can be a valuable indication of children's conceptual development. A guide to spotting 'schemas', or repeated patterns of physical movements through which children develop intellectual concepts, is included in 'Swings and roundabouts' on pages 18 to 19.

No time for breakfast

What you need

A variety of breakfast cereals, milk, bowls, porridge, syrup, honey, sugar, salt, large spoon for stirring, saucepan (transparent if possible), access to a stove.

What to do

Breakfast time is often difficult for parents and children, with parents trying to ensure that their offspring have a nourishing meal before setting off for school or nursery and children often reluctant to eat anything at all!

Re-awaken children's interest in the first meal of the day by experimenting with a variety of cereals. Involve all the senses. Can the children hear anything when the milk is poured on to the cereals? Does the texture of the cereal change when the milk is poured on? Does it make any difference whether the milk is hot or cold? Does cold cereal with milk have a particular smell? Is it different when it is hot? Which cereal do the children like best?

Try making porridge, with the children stirring the oats and water before they are heated. Let them put their hands in a small separate container of the mixture to investigate the texture. When cooked, try tasting the porridge mixed with a little salt, sugar or syrup. Which is the most popular? At each stage let the children do as much mixing, stirring and tasting as possible.

The 'sharing circle'

What you need
Paper, clear plastic wallets, string or ribbon.

What to do
Take the children into a large room, such as the hall, and ask them to sit down in a big circle. The 'sharing circle' is a format for each child to have an equal chance to share ideas or feelings without being interrupted or judged by others. The teacher might explore the children's emotions by asking, for example, 'What makes you angry?' The children could then answer in turn around the circle. Encourage them to start the sentence in the same way, for example 'I am angry when . . .'.

The teacher should always include herself as a participant, and children should be allowed to 'pass' if they wish. Shy children may want to 'pass' at first and then have their turn at the end, having gained confidence from listening to the others. Body sensations might also be explored in this way, for example 'I feel sick when . . .'. The teacher might use this information to make a class book using plastic wallets.

Can I take my cardigan off?

What you need
A collection of items to cool you down or warm you up, such as fans, hot-water bottles etc, pencils, paper.

What to do
It is a common occurrence in the nursery or school environment for children to be either too hot or too cold. Take advantage of these changes in body temperature to display a series of objects that either cool you down or warm you up, depending on the season. After discussion, the children might make their own fans to cool themselves down or make ice cubes to put in playtime drinks.

Alternatively, they could discuss how to make themselves warmer, for example, by having a warm drink, by putting clothes on a radiator or simply by putting on warmer clothing. Make class books and let the children take them home for shared reading.

When I am Hot.

I can smell chips

What you need

Old magazines, sugar paper, adhesive, paper, paints, felt-tipped pens, scissors, food essences, coffee, lemon, cologne, a rose, soap, cheese, a blindfold.

What to do

Children often show interest in food smells, especially just before lunch time. They enjoy identifying their favourite meals and usually show strong preferences and dislikes.

Build on this interest to broaden the children's repertoire of smells by making 'smelly pictures' using photographs or drawings of food, flowers, etc, sprinkled with the relevant essence or substance. The pictures could be either cut out of magazines or drawn or painted by the children. The children will have great fun identifying each other's pictures while wearing a blindfold. A temporary 'smelly picture' display could be mounted on the wall at child height.

Knickerbocker fun

What you need

Ice-cream in one or more flavours, soft fruit in season, tinned fruit, chocolate flakes, chopped nuts, hundreds and thousands, cherries, chocolate sauce, tall sundae dishes (plastic, if possible), sandwich bags and ties, rolling pin, copies of photocopiable page 95.

What to do

Children enjoy making 'concoctions', especially if they are edible. Let the children make their own individual 'knickerbocker glories' using an interesting combination of flavours and textures. Hygiene is important throughout this process, and the children should understand the need for scrupulously clean hands. Place the non-frozen ingredients on display on a low table for the children to discuss in small groups and taste small samples.

Make an illustrated ingredients sheet for shared reading. Which taste is the sweetest, crunchiest, smoothest? Can the children think of a way to crush the chocolate flakes without making a mess, for example by putting the flakes in a plastic bag, securing it with a tie and firmly rolling a rolling pin over it?

Let the children plan which ingredients they are going to include in their own special concoction, with a limit of four extras to add to the ice-cream. When the decisions have almost been reached, fetch the ice-cream out of the freezer and let it stand a few minutes to soften. Show the children the difference between trying to scoop it out while it is still frozen and after it has been left for a few minutes. Supervise closely the making and eating of the 'knickerbocker glories',

and encourage discussion wherever possible.

Follow-up

Let the children wash up any plastic dishes. Is warm water better than cold? How much washing-up liquid is needed?

When this process is over, give the children copies of photocopiable page 95 and ask them to draw their concoction, colouring in the added ingredients.

I don't feel well

What you need
Dolls teddys or other soft toys, bandages, stethoscope, thermometer (strip variety), 'pretend' blood pressure gauge and needle, paper and pencils to write prescriptions, bell, telephone for receptionist.

What to do
Arrange for a visit to a health centre, or have a doctor, health visitor or nurse visit the class to talk about her work and participate in role play, using volunteer child 'patients'. This will help to stimulate dramatic play after the visit.

Develop a simple circle game with the children sitting around you, each holding a doll or soft toy. Tell the children that you are the 'doctor' and that they should tell you what is wrong with the toy they are holding. Let them take turns in giving you a brief 'case history'.

Use the play area as a doctor's surgery, using authentic props such as real bandages and photocopied prescription sheets if possible. Let the 'doctor' have a bell to ring for the next patient to enter. Ask one child to be the doctor's receptionist, responding to phone calls and meeting the patients as they enter the waiting room. Let the children work in pairs to re-enact the patient/doctor relationship, with the doctor trying to establish what is wrong with the patient and the patient trying to describe his symptoms.

I've broken my arm

What you need
Sling, visit from a wheelchair-bound person.

What to do
Children often find it difficult to empathise with the problems of physically handicapped people. Let them experience for themselves what it is like to be handicapped by letting them put their arms in a sling for a short time (left arm in a sling for left-handers). How do they manage to draw, paint, put their coats on?

Invite a wheelchair-bound person into the school or nursery to talk to the children. Have a question time at the end of the talk for the children to express their ideas and ask questions. What would the children be unable to do if they were in a wheelchair?

Some physically handicapped people have specially adapted cars. If possible, let the children compare the differences between specially adapted and standard cars. Some taxis have been fitted with special ramps for wheelchairs. Encourage the children to compare ordinary lavatory facilities with those for the disabled.

Happy birthday!

What you need
Children's photographs, paper, a copy of *You'll soon grow into them, Titch* by Pat Hutchins (Picture Puffin).

What to do
Young children often have a very hazy idea about time. Use birthdays as an opportunity to discuss the passage of time from one year to the next. Make a special birthday book for each child using photos of previous birthday parties, and discuss the changes that have taken place in their appearance over the years.

Staff members could bring in old photographs of themselves at, say, three, four, five and six years of age. Let children talk about the differences they notice. Some may be able to put the photographs in age order.

Read *You'll soon grow into them, Titch* by Pat Hutchins and encourage the children to talk about growth. What can the children do now that they were unable to do when they were younger?

Swings and roundabouts

What you need
Indoor or outdoor play space or access to a local park or playground, adult helpers, clipboards, pens.

What to do
A visit or visits to a local park or playground can give valuable insights into children's 'schemas'. Very close observation of individual children's physical behaviour is necessary in determining a dominant schema. Therefore, the more adult helpers available for the visits, the better. If the playground is within walking distance, it may be preferable to take one small group at a time with two helpers, rather than the whole class. Explain carefully to the helpers in advance that they should make a note of any recurrent physical movements individual children seem to enjoy. A suggested 'schema observation guide' is as follows:
• Let the children run around freely on the grass, and note down any dominant movements.
• Let the children go to the playground and note especially the first piece of equipment they use, and what they do on it. Try to 'follow through' each child, observing the subsequent choice of equipment and physical movements on it. If the whole class is visiting the playground together, it is better to stagger their use of the playground, and let only one or two groups use the equipment at a time, so that the adults may clearly observe the children's movements.
• After a session on the equipment, have the children engage in a different activity (eg a visit to a pets' corner, circle

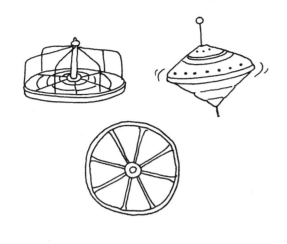

games or picnic lunch).

• If possible, let the children have a final play on the equipment, again noting which item they choose first.

Back at school, careful assessment of the notes may reveal interesting dominant schemas in some children. These can give staff ideas for further 'follow through' activities to extend and develop individuals in certain areas. These activities could take many forms, including drawings, picture- and model-making, creative floor play, fantasy and role play, action songs and rhymes and 'minute' dances.

Examples of the kinds of schemas which may be observed and possible areas of development are:

• Circular schemas – roundabouts, spinning tops, wheels.

• 'Up and down' schemas – slides, ladders, stairs, building blocks.

• 'Travelling' schemas – climbing frame, directional games, 'tracks', 'roadways', computer turtle.

• 'Swinging' schemas – swings, pendulums, waves, rocking toys, boats, hammocks.

Topsy-turvy world

What you need
Paper, collage materials, pictures of reflections in water, everyday objects.

What to do
Children enjoy looking at the world from unusual angles. Encourage their spatial awareness by playing an upside-down pairs game. Ask one child to crouch down and the other child to turn around, bend over and look at his friend through his legs. Ask the upside down child to describe both the strangeness of his friend's appearance and his surroundings. Can the children think of other ways to be upside down, such as hanging from a climbing frame or swing?

Make a topsy-turvy wall frieze with the sky at the bottom of the picture and the grass at the top. Look at pictures of reflections, in which trees and houses appear to be upside down when reflected in a lake. Examine familiar objects such as books. How can the children tell whether they are the right way up?

Play a 'What if . . .?' game in which the children consider what would happen if, for example, a post box were accidentally positioned upside down.

Discuss people and animals who are often upside down, such as trapeze artists, acrobats, bats.

Me and my family

Chapter two

This chapter focuses on children's concern with themselves in relation to family and friends, and their growing awareness of themselves as unique individuals who nonetheless share some thoughts, feelings and events with others.

Mummy's in hospital

What you need
Disinfectant, cotton wool, trolley, small blankets, plastic flowers or fruit, newspapers and magazines.

What to do
It is quite traumatic for a child to have a parent ill in hospital as it disrupts his whole daily routine and deprives him of his normal everyday love and attention. The teacher or playgroup leader needs to concentrate on the positive side of the experience, such as the excitement of visiting mummy or daddy in hospital, and perhaps taking a small present. The hospital visiting time could be re-created in the theme area with as many authentic details as possible.

Dab a small amount of disinfectant round the area to give a realistic smell of cleaning fluid. Spread out small blankets to represent beds. Provide a trolley so that the children can take turns to go round the beds delivering newspapers, books and magazines. The children will soon begin to recognise the various titles and be able to sort them into piles. Charge no more than five pence for a magazine or newspaper, with the children paying in pennies.

Mummy's having a baby

What you need
Card, fine thread, dowel or garden cane, old birthday cards, photographs of children as babies and toddlers, paper, Blu-Tack.

What to do
Faced with the arrival of a new baby in the family, young children often react with a mixture of excitement and pleasure, together with a certain amount of jealousy at being robbed of some of the parental attention. It is useful for teachers, playgroup leaders and helpers to put a positive emphasis on how the young child is going to be able to help, for example, by making a simple mobile to hang near the baby's cot. This could be made with pictures cut from birthday cards attached to a garden cane with invisible thread. Alternatively, the child could draw some bright pictures to stick on the nursery wall.

Children do not always realise that the new baby will not be an immediate playmate with built-in LEGO-building skills. Help them to become aware of the gradual stages of development by asking them to bring in a few photographs of their own babyhood and toddler days. Let them put the photographs in order of age and make them into a little booklet, attaching them to paper with Blu-Tack so that they can be replaced undamaged in the family albums. Help the children to write captions for the pictures. The booklets could then be used for shared reading, both at school and at home, and will give the child an opportunity to become used to the idea of a new sibling in the family.

Going to Gran's

What you need
Duplicating paper, clear plastic wallets, photos of grandparents and children.

What to do
Most children are very attached to their grandparents and love visiting them. Use this favourite outing to help the children gain an insight into life 50 or 60 years ago.

Send a letter home to be passed on to grandparents asking them to jot down any amusing anecdotes about events that happened in their childhood. Simplify the language of the replies, and let the children illustrate the printed anecdotes and make a class book for shared reading, using plastic wallets tied together. A collection of photographs from the grandparents' childhood would also make the children aware of differences between then and now in clothing, hairstyle and toys. Encourage the children to bring in recent photographs of themselves, so that direct comparisons can be made. Set up a display of photographs at child height with arrows matching grandparent to child.

Children often have special meals, games or treats when they visit their grandparents. A discussion using the circle format, 'When I go to Gran's I eat/play . . .', could lead to further class books being made.

Invite grandparents to the classroom to share the children's activities.

Sleeping out

What you need

An overnight case, sponge-bag, clothing and items needed for an overnight stay, eg toothbrush, flannel, pyjamas, towel, underclothes.

What to do

Children become really excited at the prospect of staying at a friend's house overnight. Turn the event into a learning experience by discussing what items of clothing will have to be packed for the visit.

What is the best way to pack a case? What will happen to the clothes if they are all jumbled together? What would the children put in the sponge-bag? Let them practise folding up clothes and packing a small overnight bag.

After an overnight visit, let them re-enact the experience in the 'pretend' corner with one child acting out the part of a mummy, or daddy, trying to persuade two very excited children to go to sleep!

Discuss packing a case for other imaginary situations, such as a trip to the moon! (See 'I can't open my bag', page 48.)

My friend's coming round

What you need
Collage materials, paper, clear plastic wallets.

What to do
Children enjoy having friends to play after school and frequently remind the teacher about it throughout the day. Ask the children involved to plan in advance what they would like to do when they get home. Can they decide on a short sequence of events? For example, they might have a snack of peanut-butter sandwiches and orange juice, watch the cartoons on television and then play outside on the climbing frame. The following day ask them to review the visit. Were they able to follow their plan or did unforeseen circumstances partially prevent them from doing so? For example, did the rain prevent them from playing outside? What did they do instead?

Investigate the friendships of children who live close to each other. Do they all play together sometimes? Make a street collage picture, labelling the houses where the children live. Do the children visit the same shops, parks, etc? Gather the groups of children together for discussion and make a short 'Neighbourhood Book'. This could contain details such as the games the children like to play in the local park or favourite sweets in the local newsagent.

Moving house

What you need
A toddletruck, a shoe box, two dolls' houses, dolls' furniture.

What to do
Moving house can be quite an upheaval for children. They are sometimes not sure what to expect, and it can be quite traumatic to see all their familiar toys and belongings being packed away. Help children come to terms with this experience by letting them act out the removal process from one house to another.

Make a simple removal van by securing a shoe box in a toddletruck. Place two dolls' houses (one full, one empty) at either end of the 'pretend' area and discuss with the children how to move the furniture from one house to the other. Which furniture should be packed in the truck first? Which items might be more delicate? Can they think of a way to stop them getting broken on the journey? Can they arrange the furniture in the correct rooms in the new house? What extra jobs will mummy and daddy have to do? How might the children help? They could put their clothes away and put their toys in their new bedrooms.

I've got new wallpaper

What you need
Cardboard box, wallpaper sample books, commercially produced dolls' house furniture, adhesive, paper, pencils, felt-tipped pens.

What to do
Children are usually very proud of their newly decorated bedrooms and sometimes even bring in a small sample of wallpaper to show the class. Help individual children to make a very simple model of their bedroom, wallpapering the inside of a cardboard box with scraps from wallpaper sample books, paper they have designed themselves or leftover paper from their newly decorated bedroom. Let the children roughly estimate how much wallpaper will be needed to cover each wall.

Discuss the position of furniture in their bedroom, and help the children to draw a very simple plan.

Furnish the box bedroom with commercially produced dolls' house furniture, encouraging the children to look at their plan as they do so.

It's nearly Christmas

What you need
A range of unusual-shaped parcels, items to be wrapped up, old wrapping paper or computer paper, adhesive tape, string, wool, paper-clips, elastic bands, small stapler, adhesive.

What to do
Children enjoy giving presents to their friends and relations and love the excitement of Christmas approaching. Use the atmosphere of festivity to let them experiment with wrapping up a variety of 'presents', in all shapes and sizes. How much wrapping paper is needed? Do they prefer adhesive tape, adhesive or string? Can the children think of other ways to wrap the presents, for example by using elastic bands, staplers or paper-clips?

Have some parcels already wrapped for the children to guess the contents, using a multi-sensory approach. Is the parcel heavy or light? Does it make a sound when gently shaken? Does it smell? Some parcels might be rather obvious, such as those containing a spade or a ball. Others might need more thought and handling, and the children might have to suggest a variety of objects that are the same shape.

Discuss choosing presents for family and friends and make a picture game with the children, matching pictures of people to suitable presents.

Brothers and sisters

What you need
No special equipment.

What to do
Most children have love/hate relationships with their siblings. Help children to explore their feelings about brothers and sisters by using the circle format to share opinions, for example, 'I like him when . . .' or 'I am cross when she . . .'.

Compare brothers and sisters. If the nursery shares the same site as the infant building, invite an older sibling to the classroom for a few minutes.

Once in a while, staff find themselves teaching identical twins. Enlist the children's help to find instant ways of identifying each twin. Discuss the similarities and differences between the twins.

Come to our party

What you need
Ingredients for simple party food, paper, felt-tipped pens.

What to do
Children love going to parties, and their excitement and interest is heightened if they are fully involved in the planning and preparation. Plan an end of term party in which the children make an invitation to give to the parent or minder who collects them from school.

Have a survey to help determine their favourite party food and drinks. Emphasise the notion of hospitality with the children, letting them consider the type of food that would be enjoyed by both parents and children, for example, cocktail sausages. Spend time preparing easy party snacks and encourage the children to estimate the amount of ingredients needed. Do not forget to mention the necessity of having clean hands before handling food. Involve the children in setting and decorating the table.

I'm tired today

What you need
Paper, clear plastic wallets, ribbon, duplicating paper, crayons, felt-tipped pens.

What to do
Most young children have some sort of regular bedtime ritual involving perhaps a bath, brushing teeth, a story and going to bed with a favourite cuddly toy. One idea for exploring these rituals is to take the children into a large space and use the circle format to give every child a chance to discuss his bedtime routine without being interrupted. For example, proceed around the circle asking each child to complete the sentence: 'I go to bed with my . . .'.

Let the children draw a picture of their favourite cuddly toy and help them to write the captions. Insert the pictures into plastic wallets, and tie them with ribbon to make a book. Each evening a different child can take the book home.

An alternative title could be 'Our favourite bedtime rhymes' or 'Our favourite bedtime stories' (eg Gemma likes her dad to read *The Three Bears*).

Let the children take home a photocopy of a clockface for parents and children to fill in at bedtime (to the nearest hour). Use the results to make a class chart to find out the most popular time for going to bed. Is it the children who go to bed the latest who are always saying 'I'm tired'? Can the children think of a suitable solution to this problem?

'I go to bed with my . . . .'

The wheels on the bus

What you need
Toy buses, coaches or minibuses, junk boxes for model making, adhesive, adhesive tape, string, rectangular table, cushions, toy steering wheel, jacket, peaked cap, tin foil.

What to do
Some children are used to travelling only in cars, and a bus ride may be quite a novelty for them. Take advantage of this interest by letting children explore different forms of bus travel, such as single-decker buses, double-decker buses, minibuses, long coaches and short coaches. Set up a classroom exhibition of both commercially produced toy buses and coaches and homemade ones made of boxes stuck together.

Take small well-supervised groups of children to watch a main road and see how many different types of coaches or buses go by.

Most nurseries and schools have at least one annual outing on a coach. Use an inspection of the vehicle as an integral part of the trip and afterwards try to re-create the coach journey in the play area using a sturdy table, cushions and a toy steering wheel. The 'driver' could be dressed in a jacket with shiny buttons and a special hat, created by using an old cap and fixing a band of card around the outside with a shiny official-looking badge of foil on the front. If time and resources are scarce, badges stuck on with adhesive tape are an instant way of giving dressing-up clothes a touch of authentic detail which children appreciate.

On the right track

What you need

Plenty of willing helpers, toy train set, sugar paper, boxes, construction toy for signals, card, adhesive, scissors, small suitcase, play people.

What to do

Many young children are familiar with some train vocabulary, thanks to *Thomas the Tank Engine*, but are unfamiliar with the experience of going to a station and actually riding on a train. Send a letter to parents, outlining the plan for a short journey departing from a local station and continuing for a few stops, with, possibly, a picnic before the return journey. Let the children experience at firsthand the hustle and bustle of a busy station with its accompanying sounds and smells. Visit the buffet, watch the notice board change as the trains arrive and depart and listen to the voice of the station announcer.

How do people move heavy suitcases around? How does the train driver know when everyone is safely aboard? Let the children have their tickets punched by the ticket inspector. What is the difference between their tickets and a platform ticket? Can the children guess why platform tickets are necessary? Are there any reserved seats on the train? Can the children think of any other occasion when seats are reserved? (See also 'Tickets please', page 78)

Back in the classroom, allow the children to re-create the experience in the play area using train tracks, play people and boxes to represent the buffet, ticket office, etc. Can the children find a way to make a signal go up and down?

Let the children solve the real problem of moving a heavy suitcase.

Form a human 'train' for outdoor play, with the children holding onto each other's waists and following directional instructions.

Departures		Arrivals
Flight	time	11.40
03.03	09.30	12.30
05.17	10.40	01.10
08.42	12.50	

Fasten your seat belts

What you need
Two small suitcases, chairs, belts, paper, felt-tipped pens, stapler, large box, old passports, ink stamp, small trolley, perfume boxes, sugar paper.

What to do
In these days of package holidays children often experience air travel at quite an early age. Re-create this experience in your classroom by setting up an 'airport'. Inform parents of your project and many will be happy to send in old passports and other items connected with air travel such as luggage labels and old tickets. Let the children examine the passports closely, paying particular attention to photographs, stamped information and details about the passport holder. Then let them make their own using little booklets of paper stapled together and an ink stamp. They can draw in a 'photograph' and write down their age.

Comparisons can be made between two similar suitcases, one heavy and one light. Use the side of a large box to display the times of arrival and departure, in clock faces as well as digits.

Arrange chairs in pairs to represent the inside of an aeroplane. Loosely attach ordinary belts as seat belts. Let a pair of children wheel a small trolley up and down, displaying 'duty-free goods' priced in pennies. Make a few signs to stick up round the play area, such as No Smoking and Fasten Your Seat Belts.

Pairs of children can play at being air-traffic controllers and pilots, taking turns to follow directional instructions in the playground or in a large space.

I go to ballet

What you need
Plastic wallets, collection of objects associated with hobbies and clubs.

What to do
Many children attend out-of-school activities such as ballet, Tumble Tots and gymnastics. Improve and reinforce links between home and school by encouraging the children to share their interests with other children and teachers. This can be done by making an instant 'book', with all the children drawing a picture of their favourite after-school activity and slipping it into a plastic wallet. Bind them together and let each child in turn take the book home to share with their parents.

Alternatively, organise a miming game where the children have to guess the nature of each other's after-school activities.

Time could be allotted for individual children to 'teach' a partner their new skill, making sure they give clear, simple instructions.

These ideas can be particularly helpful in drawing out a fairly quiet, shy child who is slow to share information about his home life.

My treasures

Chapter three

Allowing favourite possessions to be brought to school provides a tangible link between home life and school and encourages conversation, especially with shy children. The teacher is given an insight into the child's personal interests, and the 'treasure' can provide the catalyst for many conversations and activities. Bringing toys to school is a good way of extending home interests. Children are helped to see new uses for toys and encouraged to share their belongings and respect the property of others. The play value of equipment is enhanced, for example, when space figures from home are used with bricks or sand from the classroom.

It is important for nursery and infant staff to discuss ways of exploiting the learning potential of toys from home and of school equipment. For example, jigsaws can be used in a variety of ways: pairs of children can sort out two jumbled jigsaws encouraging observation and co-operation.

I've got new shoes

What you need

Shoe-box lid, sticky dot labels, children's gym shoes in different sizes, felt-tipped pen, a variety of children's shoes, some new and some old, a visit from a shoe mender.

What to do

One place that all children need to visit every few months is a shoe shop, and children are often intrigued by the measuring devices used by the shop assistants.

Set up a 'shoe shop' in the classroom using a shoe-box lid as a simple foot gauge. Using the correct sizes and half-sizes of children's feet, colour code the gauge with sticky dot labels with the appropriate size written on. Attach matching dots to a few pairs of children's gym shoes. There should be a large enough variety of size within the class for some shoes to be too small, some too large and some that fit comfortably! The children can take turns to be the customer and the shop assistant, who measures the child's feet on the gauge and is able to predict confidently 'You need this size shoe', by looking at the colour stickers or by reading the number on the gauge.

Let the children make a display of shoes ranging from those that are brand new to those that are worn out. Discuss what happens to shoes that are worn all the time. For example, the ends become scuffed and holes sometimes appear on the soles. How can we protect the leather on shoes? Arrange for a shoe repairer to visit the classroom. Talk about the different parts of a shoe, such as tongue, sole and heel. Let the children compare the tongue of a shoe with their own tongues. Are there any similarities?

My new game

What you need
Child's game from home.

What to do
Children love playing 'winning' games. Use this interest to develop extended conversations with individual children, in which they explain the rules of their particular game from home. Ensure that it is one that they have already played a few times with parents, siblings and friends. Accept invented rules as long as they make sense. Follow up the conversation by encouraging the children to 'teach' the rules to a classmate before they play the game together.

I've got some felt-tipped pens

What you need
Felt-tipped pens, colour charts, ordering tray.

What to do
Most children love using felt-tipped pens, enjoying the vividness of the colours. Use this interest in colour to encourage the children to sort out the different shades from light to dark using an 'ordering tray'.

Collect some colour charts from DIY shops and see if the children can match the felt-tipped pens to the colours on the chart. Discuss the unusual colour names on the chart. Can the children think of other unusual names for colours? (See also 'Living colour', page 74)

Look at my diamond

What you need
Costume jewellery, curtain rings, macaroni, lentils, pulses, card, scissors, adhesive, string, wooden beads.

What to do
Children often think that all precious stones are diamonds. Hire some jewellery from a theatrical agency or amateur theatre, or buy some cheap costume jewellery. Discuss the names and colours of the stones, eg emerald green and ruby red. Encourage the children to play kings and queens, wearing plenty of jewels.

Make up a class story about some jewels that are stolen or a secret treasure that is found.

Let the children put curtain rings in order of size and necklaces in order of length.

Set up a jewellery shop in the 'pretend' corner, using costume jewellery brought from home and jewellery made by the children, for example, pendants made by sticking lentils and pulses on to circular card discs or necklaces made of threaded macaroni or wooden beads.

My new skipping rope

What you need
Skipping ropes, posters, information books on activities using ropes.

What to do
Children often bring skipping ropes to school for use at playtime. Encourage the children to think divergently by proposing new ways of using a skipping rope, for example as horses' reins or laid along the ground as a tightrope. Let them try this, in small groups or pairs. Stress that they should never put ropes around their own or anyone else's neck.

Organise a rope search in which the children look for pictures of ropes being used in real life, such as in mountaineering. They will soon become aware of the fact that rope is made use of on television programmes and in adventure films.

Use simple books and posters to create a display about the use of rope.

I've got a new car

What you need
Toy cars, car brochures, wooden or plastic bricks, paper, skipping ropes, train track, access to a new car.

What to do
Children become very excited if their parents buy a new car. Use this enthusiasm to help the children's discriminatory and sorting skills. Set up a toy car exhibition, giving the children plenty of opportunities to sort the cars by colour, shape and size. Collect some brochures from car showrooms and encourage the children to match the cars to the pictures.

Help the children to build a car park using toy bricks, and encourage them to match the number of cars to the number of spaces, possibly numbering each space to develop number recognition. Make simple signs such as 'Car Park Full'.

A smooth wooden train track or skipping ropes can be used to create a motorway system, even incorporating a spaghetti junction.

Allow small groups of children to inspect closely a real new car, and introduce the children to the different parts. You may be surprised at the information already picked up by the young enthusiasts!

Can the children read the number plates of cars? Compare a toy car with a real car. What details have been left off the bodywork of the toy version?

Snowy goes to school

What you need
A variety of children's pets.

What to do
Children are often very attached to their family pets and play an important part in looking after them. Let the children share their expertise with the whole class by occasionally allowing them to bring their pet into school. Send home a letter well in advance, asking for parental permission to borrow the pet for a short time, explaining that dogs, cats and other large animals are best accompanied by an adult. The parent and child can then talk with the class about caring for the family pet and can demonstrate how to brush the dog, etc. Ideally the classroom should already have a pet animal, but this method introduces some variety, involves parents and allows children the opportunity to speak in front of the class about their own special pet, thus increasing their self-confidence.

Make sure that children who are allergic are kept at a distance from the animal.

Sticker fun

What you need
Folded paper, large freezer labels, a commercially produced sticker album, scissors, adhesive, paper, felt-tipped pens, catalogues and magazines.

What to do
Many children are fascinated by the idea of collecting pictures for a sticker album. Bring a sticker album into school for the children to examine and discuss what would be needed to make a sticker booklet to give to a friend. Emphasise individual interests, for example, a child might cut out four different pictures of cars from a catalogue and stick them to the front of four large, numbered freezer labels. She can then give them to a friend to stick in a pre-prepared booklet with window squares labelled 1, 2, 3 and 4. He simply has to match the numbered pictures to the numbered windows. The booklets might have titles such as 'My Sticker Book of Cars' or 'My Sticker Book of Toys'.

To the rescue!

What you need
Dolls, puppets, teddy bears, Play people, construction kits, Plasticine, twigs, coloured tissue paper.

What to do
Children enjoy bringing puppets and dolls into school but do not always get the full play value out of them, tending either to leave them lying around or to wander around all day clutching them.

Use these toys to full advantage by allowing them to enhance creative floor play and story-telling. Small dolls and action figures can be used together with bricks, Duplo etc, for the children to make up their own adventure stories, based on favourite television programmes or stories that they have heard. Try using a doll and three teddy bears to re-create Goldilocks and the Three Bears, making the bowls of porridge out of Plasticine and the chairs and beds out of construction toys.

The dolls and play figures can also be used for creative problem-solving. For example, what is the best way for the doll to escape from the fierce tiger in the jungle (made of twigs stuck in Plasticine)? Can the children make a ladder high enough to rescue the doll from the 'burning' house (use coloured tissue for flames and pieces from a construction kit for the ladder)?

Secret treasures

What you need
A variety of locks and keys, padlocks, money boxes with keys, small toys, minute timer, tricycle, toys, catalogues, scissors, black card.

What to do
Children enjoy keeping their treasures under lock and key and like to lock and unlock the container to check that they are safe.

Ask parents to send in old containers with locks, keys and padlocks. After marking the keys and locks to ensure that the correct key is eventually returned to each lock, let the children experiment to find out if the keys can be used on different locks. Can they think of a reason why this is usually not the case? Set up a working display of money boxes and their keys. Can the children match the correct key to each lock? Put a small surprise in each box. Time how long it takes each child to open all the locks. Can they beat the minute timer?

Can the children work out the best way to secure the tricycle so that it will not be stolen? Let them experiment by using the padlock on different parts of the tricycle. Adult help may be necessary to close the padlock. Do any of the children think of securing the tricycle to a heavy object?

Set up a table with about five popular toys and collect large pictures of the same toys from magazines and catalogues. Cut out keyhole shapes from a piece of black card and place them over the pictures. Encourage the children to use simple logic to identify the pictures by comparing the section they can see with the toys on the table.

A harder version would be to use just the picture and the keyhole card.

Transformers

What you need

Fans, concertina, umbrella, sunbed, flat-pack box, cocktail umbrellas, folding Christmas decorations, paper, scissors, construction toys such as Mobilo.

What to do

Children derive a lot of play value from toys that transform from one shape to another. Introduce them to the wonders of design technology by exploring everyday objects that change shape, such as a flat-pack box that has to be folded into shape, an umbrella that has to be opened, a fan that unfolds or a sunbed that folds up flat. On a smaller scale, let the children play with cocktail umbrellas to observe the mechanism of the umbrella going up and down.

Can the children design their own transformers using a variety of paper and construction toys? Because of its flexibility, Mobilo is a useful construction toy for making transforming machines.

Let the children experiment by cutting patterns in folded paper and unfolding the paper for the final result. Cutting out half-figures on the edge of a piece of paper that has been folded a few times results in a row of figures, all holding hands. Show the children how the same principle applies to paper Christmas decorations.

I can't open my bag

What you need
A variety of adult bags, camping equipment, paper, felt-tipped pens.

What to do
'I can't open my bag' is a frequent cry in a busy reception-class cloakroom. Do a survey of the children's school bags. Which fastening is the most popular? Make a chart. Let the children practise opening and shutting each other's bags. Which fastening is the easiest to deal with? Can the children think of reasons why? Extend the exploration into the fastenings on adult-sized bags, such as a duffle bag, a sports holdall and a rucksack. Look at the design of each bag. Can the children give valid reasons for the shape and size and material for each bag? For example, a sports bag often has a separate compartment for tennis, badminton or squash rackets. A swimming bag is often lined with plastic inside to hold wet towels.

Use some of the bags for imaginative play. What equipment would the children pack in a rucksack for a week's camping holiday? Set out a table of equipment and clothes, some suitable, some not suitable. What might a mountaineer pack in his rucksack in case of emergency? Why is a rucksack carried on a walker's back?

I've got my ten-metre badge

What you need
Child's ten-metre swimming badge, metre sticks, bean bags, bowl of goldfish.

What to do
Children are proud to show off their out-of-school achievements by bringing in badges and certificates of merit. One of the most common out-of-school activities is swimming, and children are often heard to say, 'I've got my ten-metre badge'.

To a non-swimming child this distance means very little, and even the badge-holder can find it difficult to relate the distance swum to that on dry land. Ask the children to estimate ten metres along a corridor, then use metre sticks to measure out the distance. How many children lying head to toe will stretch across ten metres? How many giant strides cover ten metres? Have a pairs competition to see which child can cover the distance in the fewest strides. Help them to measure the distance using the metre sticks.

Let the badge-holder lie across a bench and demonstrate the swimming stroke she used to gain the badge. Do the children know the movements and names of the other strokes?

Observe a bowl of goldfish. How do they move through the water?

Look at my shells

What you need
A variety of shells, decorated paper plates or small foil-covered trays, sand tray.

What to do
After the summer holidays many children return to school clutching bags of sandy shells. Develop the children's sorting skills by encouraging them to set up an attractive exhibition of shells using decorated paper plates or small trays covered with foil. Let the children give reasons for choosing a favourite shell. Use the circle format in small groups for the children to say, 'This shell is my favourite because it reminds me of . . .'.

Separate the halves of bivalve shells and ask the children if they can match them up. Use the shells to decorate a beach scene in the sand tray or to make sequence patterns across the outdoor sand pit.

People and places

Chapter four

The importance of structured imaginative play in organising a child's experience is now well recognised. Fantasy and role play enable a child to select, re-order and explore aspects of life she may have found puzzling, pleasurable, painful or exciting. It is of great benefit to the children if, through informal contact with parents, staff have knowledge of the kinds of 'grown up' jobs and leisure time interests the children may be familiar with. A genuine question on the part of a staff member to a child about the progress of the family's tropical fish can give rise to an extended conversation about looking after fish, and can be a definite boost to a child's self-esteem.

Sometimes, school life can appear divorced from 'real life' to children. For this reason, every opportunity should be used to take the children on visits to workplaces and to invite workers into school so that children can talk with adults about their work, interests and hobbies.

I've drunk all my milk

What you need
Milk crate, bottles, straws, a visit from a milkman, milkman's cap (see 'The wheels on the bus', page 23), money satchel, note book, toddletruck, string, pedal car, plastic milk bottles or empty milk cartons, cardboard dividers from wine boxes, empty boxes.

What to do
The comment 'I've drunk all my milk!', frequently heard at milk time, can lead to exploring the role of the milkman. Many children are very interested in the 'emptiness' of the bottle ('all gone') and enjoy putting bottles in order of 'emptiness' (or amount of milk left). There is also the fascination of the crate itself, which can give rise to much valuable discussion about one-to-one matching, using small plastic bottles or empty cartons.

Invite a milkman to visit to talk about his job (the early mornings, collecting money, problems with birds pecking at bottle tops – do the children have any solutions?). Let the children inspect the float, while reminding them never to play near one.

Such input will give rise to enriched fantasy and role play. Prepare the children by making up a class poem, incorporating appropriate sounds (hum of float, clatter of crate, clink of bottles) and miming actions of the milkman (lifting crates and bottles, opening gates, driving, ringing doorbells). Provide an appropriate hat and money satchel, and use a note book as the milkman's order book. A milk float can be made by placing the cardboard dividers from a wine carton inside a toddletruck. Fill it

with plastic bottles or empty milk cartons. Tie the toddletruck to the back of a pedal car with string. Play games in the playground in which the milkman must drive and stop at various 'houses'. 'Houses' can simply be outlined in chalk on the playground or on a wall, each with a number. Leave a note outside each 'house', telling the milkman how many bottles to leave.

Look at my postcard

What you need
Used postcards, letters, card, stamps, wrapping from parcels, dressing-up clothes to represent a postman's uniform, roll of wallpaper, two empty tin foil boxes, corrugated cardboard, poster paint.

What to do
Enthusiasm for a 'postman's exhibition' consisting of letters, cards, leaflets and parcels can be sparked off by one child bringing in a colourful postcard. Many children comment that they rarely receive personal mail (except on their birthdays). As a surprise, send a postcard or letter to each child at home, to arrive on a Saturday. Ask them to bring in any old envelopes, postcards etc, for a 'postman's exhibition on Monday'.

Take the children to see a letter box at collection time, have a chat with the postman, and look at his van. Ask the children why they think there is a grille in the box. Many children are intrigued by the physical act of 'posting' things through holes and flaps.

Make a wall frieze of painted doors on the back of a length of wallpaper, and let the children decide on a street name for it. Make a 'letter box' for each door, using a corrugated cardboard flap and adhesive tape, and paint a number on each door. Make the frieze stand out a little from the wall by attaching each end of the wallpaper to empty tin foil boxes, fixed to the wall with drawing pins. Let the children take turns to be the postman delivering a small number of letters and postcards, correctly matching the door number to the address. (See also 'Letters', page 89.)

Let's call the police

What you need
Contact with local police station, squared paper, black felt-tipped pens, adhesive tape, card, paints, clear self-adhesive film, clipboard, pencil, cuddly toys or pictures of pet animals.

What to do
Arrange for a policeman, or policewoman, to visit the class to talk about the job, and let the children look at the police car or motorbike. Such a visit will inspire much imaginative play.

Improvise police uniforms by adding black and white checked strips of paper to ordinary clothes. Cover these paper strips with clear self-adhesive film prior to attaching them to the clothes with adhesive tape. Similarly, ordinary 'sit'n'ride' vehicles can be instantly transformed into police vehicles by adding black and white strips and 'Police' signs to them.

Follow-up
'I've lost my pet' is a circle game which helps observation, memory and oral skills. Let one child sit in the centre of a small circle of children. Tell the other children that he is a policeman and, if possible, let him wear an appropriate hat and carry a clipboard and pencil. Prior to sitting down, ask a second child to look at a collection of cuddly toys or pictures of pets, choose one, and try to remember what it looks like. This child must then give a description of his 'lost pet' to the policeman, who 'writes' down its description. From the description, the policeman must guess the animal. If he guesses correctly, he changes places with the other child.

What a queue!

What you need
Small roll of paper, black felt-tipped pen, tissue boxes, scissors, paper cups, or magazine pictures of food, models, plastic crockery, card, clear self-adhesive film, toy or real money, toy cash register or divided money tray, rounders post.

What to do
Many entertaining 'queuing' games can be devised, which can also introduce the concept of ordinal number. For example, in the shopping corner, hang up a roll of home-made perforated tickets, numbered one to ten. As the children queue up at the counter, let each one take a ticket, simulating the practice of some supermarkets and shops to avoid queue-jumping.

Children enjoy queuing up in a 'self-service café'. Use cut down tissue boxes as trays. Make a simple illustrated menu wallchart. Place several tables end to end, and let the children slide their 'trays' along as they choose their 'food'. 'Food' can be made from dough or cut from magazine pictures stuck on card and covered in clear self-adhesive film. At the end of the row of tables, have a 'cashier' behind a cash register.

Follow-up
Make a 'bus stop' by attaching a circular piece of card on to a rounders post. Children queue at the stop. The 'bus' (one or more children) comes along and stops, and the driver shouts out the number of children who may get on board. Holding on to each other's clothes, the 'bus' sets off again, going faster and faster around the playground, slowing down when it reaches the bus stop again.

Bonny babies

What you need

Small washing-up bowl, small cardboard box, sugar paper, scissors, white card, felt-tipped pens, split pin, washing-up bowl, three plastic baby bottles, white powder paint, dolls, baby clothes, white flannels with Velcro tabs sewn on for 'nappies', white shirts, baby bath, baby toiletries.

What to do

The birth of a baby brother or sister can provide the stimulus for one of the most popular themes in the school, the baby clinic. Take the children to a clinic, or arrange for a clinic nurse or health visitor to visit. At the same time, invite a mother with a young baby, so the nurse, mother and baby can role play in front of the children, the nurse talking through with the children what she is checking and why. If possible, ask the mother to bath her baby in front of the class.

Turn a corner of the classroom into a 'waiting area' with chairs, baby toys and magazines, and an 'examination room' with baby scales.

If scales cannot be borrowed from a clinic or chemist, then a very simple version can be made. Cover a small cardboard box with sugar paper. Invert it, stick a white circle on one side and draw on numbers to represent a dial. Fix a card 'needle' on to this 'dial', using a split pin. Place a small washing-up bowl on top. 'Babies' can then be placed in the bowl, and the doctor or nurse can announce how many kilograms the baby weighs, moving the hand accordingly. Let the children write the weight on baby 'weight cards'.

The 'babies' can be weighed each day, becoming heavier each time.

Staff should interact with children in the 'baby clinic', taking on roles as mother (describing baby's symptoms to child 'doctor'), nurse or doctor (asking 'mother' how much milk baby has at each feed, etc).

Use three plastic baby bottles, to help children understand the concepts of 'full', 'half empty' and 'empty'. Make a weak solution of white powder paint and water for 'milk'. Fill one bottle completely, fill another bottle half full, and put a few drops in the third bottle to denote an 'empty' bottle. Use the plastic discs provided, underneath the teats, to ensure that the bottles do not leak. The children will enjoy 'feeding' their babies, holding up the bottles to discuss now much has been taken. Discuss that fact that many babies are breast fed.

Fire! Fire!

What you need

Contact with a fire station, egg-timer, toy telephones, gloves, wellingtons, firefighter's helmet, cardboard axe, goggles, old vacuum cleaner hose or hose pipe, sit'n'ride vehicle, card, felt-tipped pens, adhesive tape, gummed paper.

What to do

Take the opportunity of using your fire practice to introduce a fire brigade theme. Use a one-, two- or three-minute egg-timer to see how quickly the children can vacate the room. Repeat this several times to see how good they become at beating the egg-timer.

If possible, arrange a visit to a fire station. In subsequent structured play, make use of telephone dialogue, in which children must dial 999, and say where the fire is and how it started. Develop the concept of speed: can the firefighters beat the egg timer as they change into helmet, jacket, gloves and boots?

Improvise firefighters' clothes by sticking badges and signs on to dressing-up clothes. Take a plastic police helmet and cover the badge with a yellow star shape made from gummed paper. Stick a 'Fire Brigade' sign to the side of a sit'n'ride vehicle with adhesive tape.

Come in, number four

What you need
Inflatable paddling pool, junk items for model boats, Play people, soil, twigs, cake tin.

What to do
A child's visit to a boating lake can spark off a 'boating lake' theme, which can provide an imaginative context for floating and sinking activities. Use an inflatable paddling pool, either indoors or outside, as the boating lake. Put water in to a depth of a few inches. Supervise the children closely when they play with the paddling pool.

Encourage them to think about what items they can use from the modelling area to make boats which will float (eg polystyrene trays, date boxes etc). Add Play people. Number the boats, and let the children be the 'boat owners', calling for example, 'Come in, number four,' etc. Such games give opportunities for introducing terms such as floating, sinking, heavy, light, forwards, backwards, round and round, fast, slow.

Discuss with the children their ideas for making an 'island' in the middle of the lake, possibly out of mud, with twigs for trees. How might they stop the island from dissolving in the water (eg build the island on an upturned shallow dish, so it is above the water)?

Buckets and spades

What you need

Holiday photographs, postcards, clear plastic wallets and ribbon, sugar paper, shells, dish of salty water, sandpaper, beach requisites (sunglasses etc), light brown towels, buckets, spades, dolls, quoits, beach ball, toy fish, blue fabric.

What to do

A child's excited comments about her seaside holiday can give rise to a wealth of linguistic and exploratory play. Ask children to bring in holiday photographs and postcards, and let them draw pictures of their holiday experiences. Stick the pictures on to white paper, and place them in plastic wallets to make an instant 'Our holidays' book.

Make a three-dimensional rebus for children to look at, listen to, touch, taste and smell. Jot down what the children say about the seaside, such as 'We see the shiny sun. We touch the tickly sand, taste the salty water, hear the donkeys' bells.' Write out their comments on a large piece of sugar paper, leaving spaces for appropriate pictures and objects for children to handle. Place the paper on a table for children to 'read' and discuss with an adult.

Help the children to improvise a dance in which they express the movement of waves with their bodies. Let them hold hands to form a long wave, use their feet and arms to suggest waves moving 'forward and back, forward and back, higher, higher and over'.

Make a collection of different-sized buckets. Let the children put them in size order.

Make a display of the items contained in a beach bag.

Make an indoor 'beach', using light brown towels, or, in summer, use an outdoor sand pit with buckets and spades. Use blue fabric next to the 'beach' to represent the sea, with beach balls, toy fish and dolls wearing quoits as rubber rings.

Splashing around

What you need
Water trough, sink, play people, plastic guttering, straws, Blu-Tack, plastic flowers and leaves, dolls' house chairs and tables, paper umbrellas, small plastic ruler and Mobilo ladders for 'diving boards'.

What to do
Many children have been taken to swimming 'water worlds' that have exciting features such as wave machines, chutes, jacuzzis and jungle foliage. Describing such a visit can provide a stimulating challenge to a child's imaginative and problem-solving skills as he creates a 'water world' in the water trough.

Discuss with the children what items they could use. For example, a plastic ruler could be used as a diving board, while guttering or a miniature slide could become a water chute. How can they make a jacuzzi? If a sink is used, allow the children to let one tap run gently as a 'waterfall', and let them blow through straws to simulate a jacuzzi.

As the children use their play people in the 'water world', encourage the development of their scientific thinking within an imaginative framework. For example, 'This little girl is jumping off a low diving board, and this little girl is jumping off the high diving board. Who do you think will make the bigger splash?'

Tapping away

What you need

Contact with the school secretary, items with keys to press, such as a toy telephone, toy trumpet, calculator, piano keyboard, typewriter, computer; toothpaste cartons, small white freezer labels, felt-tipped pen, woodwork bench, hammer, nails, wood, chime bars, ingredients for a soft dough, sand.

What to do

In today's push-button society, so much is available literally at one's fingertips. Be on the alert for opportunities for exploiting and developing children's finger play.

Arrange for the children to visit the school secretary working at her typewriter or word processor. Make a display of items with keys to press, such as telephones, calculators, computers, trumpet and a piano keyboard. Encourage the children to make their own telephones using a toothpaste carton and small white freezer labels, with numbers written in felt-tipped pen. Children who know their telephone numbers could 'press' the keys.

Develop the many and varied finger rhymes and songs which involve making tapping gestures. Provide opportunities for hammering at the woodwork bench and tapping out rhythms on drums and chime bars. Let the children make a soft dough and make finger holes in it — a very satisfying feeling. Alternatively, use wet sand. Let the children look closely at the width of each hole and match it to the appropriate finger.

Extend the finger awareness project to toes. Organise a demonstration of tap dancing, perhaps from a parent or an older child. Let the children make footprints in damp sand.

Child's view of the world

Chapter five

Research* has shown that often the child who is intensely curious at home and is forever asking 'why?' may not do so at nursery or in the reception class. Staff can do much to remedy this by trying to make time for extended conversations with individuals and small groups and by finding out as much as they can about children's interests outside school. In order to help a child come to understand the world around him, it is vital to arrange as many opportunities as possible for firsthand experiences. Let the children go outside to look at, listen to, feel, smell and, if appropriate, taste natural aspects of the world in order to stimulate conversation.

Young Children Learning Professor B Tizard and M Hughes (Fontana).

Why?

What you need
No special requirements.

What to do
When children first start school, shyness can inhibit them from asking the questions they would freely ask at home. Some children never quite overcome this and do not become the fully active, questioning learners they could be.

An amusing 'ice-breaking' language game is 'Why?' Play with individual children to encourage them to overcome their shyness and ask questions. Encourage the child to say 'why' in response to everything you say. The dialogue may go something like this:

Adult: On my way to school this morning I had to buy some eggs.
Child: Why?
Adult: Because I dropped some this morning and they broke all over the kitchen floor.
Child: Why?
Adult: Because I overslept.
Child: Why?
Adult: Why do *you* think?
Older children may enjoy having the roles reversed!

It's pouring down

What you need

Play people, toy buildings, toy cars, water trough, LEGO, cocktail umbrellas, polythene, sprays, squeezy bottles, nozzles, eye droppers, rubber shower tap attachment set, hoses, garden sprinkler, tubing, watering cans, kettles, jugs, teapots and coffee pots with different spouts, tea strainers, sieves, sponges, paint, paper.

What to do

Children are fascinated by the phenomenon of water falling in different ways. Whenever possible, let the children go outside, suitably clad, to experience for a couple of minutes the sensation of rain falling. Let them watch it fall from the sky into pipes, gutters and grids. Look at the drips falling off leaves and trickling down window panes. Let them listen to rain falling on a metal tray, and encourage them to put out their hands and tongues to feel and taste it. Draw their attention to the smell of damp grass, leaves, soil and bark.

Talk about rain 'spitting, drizzling, showering, pouring and bucketing down'. Let the children use play people, toy buildings, cars and LEGO to re-create in an empty water trough their own three-dimensional rainy day. Cover cocktail umbrellas with polythene for the play people to carry. Ask the children why the polythene is necessary. Let the children use a variety of water containers and pourers to 'make it rain' on the town. For example, they could use eye droppers for 'spitting' rain, a squeezy bottle for 'drizzle', a child's watering can for 'rain showers', and children's teapots for 'pouring' rain. Talk about puddles and reflections, and let the children 'drive' toy cars through the rain, splashing the play people! Let the children re-create a thunderstorm, with sound effects, and a subsequent flood, requiring the play people to be rescued in lifeboats.

Follow-up
Let the children make 'rainfall patterns' on paper, using paint and eye droppers, squeezy bottles and watering cans. During the summer, children can make water patterns, pictures and words on paving stones, using washing-up liquid bottles, watering can, etc.

The sun's in my eyes

What you need
Paints, brushes, paper, lamp or torch, card, scissors.

What to do
Young children frequently complain about the sun being in their eyes. Ask for ideas on how to deal with this. Talk about shade and standing in the shade.

Show them how the same colour looks light when in the sunlight, and dark when in the shade. Ask the children to paint a sunny day picture. Shine a lamp or torch on to the picture to simulate sunlight, then pass a small cardboard cut-out of a cloud in front of the lamp to show how the colours in the picture appear darker. Repeat this several times.

I slipped on the ice

What you need
Used tin foil food containers, food colouring, dry leaves, ice-cube moulds, lolly and jelly moulds, fruit juices, balloons, freezer, water trough, play people, small boats.

What to do
An icy morning provides an exhilarating start to the day. Ask the children to show you the icy patches they have turned into slides and talk about icy patches and freezing.

Let the children make their own puddle experiments. Squash foil pie dishes into puddle shapes and fill them with water, to which you have added food colouring and a few small dry leaves. Leave the 'puddles' outside overnight to freeze. Talk about how the shape of the frozen puddle is moulded to the shape of the container. Develop this idea by making ice-cubes and ice lollies (with fresh fruit juice), and making 'ice balloons'. Fill a strong balloon with water, coloured with food colouring, by holding the balloon over the end of a tap. Let children feel the weight of the water in the balloon. Tie the neck of the water-filled balloon, and leave it in a freezer overnight, then remove the balloon by making a slit with scissors and carefully peeling it off. Let the children look at patterns in the ice. Place the ice balloon in a trough of warm water and let the children watch and listen to the ice cracking up as they pour water over it. As the ice balloon breaks up into realistic 'icebergs', the children will enjoy sailing small boats around them. Add play people, model penguins or polar bears.

The ice is all gone!

What you need
Old tin foil food containers, small loaf of bread, cardboard box, black felt-tipped pen, small white freezer labels.

What to do
Children can be dismayed to discover that their favourite early morning ice patch 'slide' has vanished by lunchtime! Talk about thawing. Leave the tin foil 'puddles' from the previous activity outside over a period of several days to demonstrate freezing and thawing.

Bring in a small loaf of bread, freeze it, then thaw it, using the word 'defrost'. Ask the children how we could defrost the bread more quickly if we were in a hurry.

Many children will know about the 'defrost' programme on a microwave oven, and will enjoy making their own 'microwave' for the home corner, using a cardboard box and white sticky labels. Using this 'microwave' in domestic role play with adults can give rise to valuable number recognition and an understanding of 'high', 'medium' and 'low' heat.

It nearly blew me over

What you need
Toothpicks, paper, water trough, polystyrene food containers, wooden lollipop sticks, paper, straws, small plastic balls, two balloon pumps, two foot pumps, balloons.

What to do
Take the children outside on a windy day, and let them feel themselves being pushed by the wind. Talk about gusts, breezes, gales and hurricanes.

Many enjoyable activities can be devised for pairs of children involving simple 'blowing' races. Children could make very simple sail boats with polystyrene food containers, paper and toothpicks and blow them along themselves, or use a balloon pump.

A very simple version of 'blow football' may be made using two straws and a small plastic ball on a tray.

Twigs and flowers

What you need
Branches in bud, spring flowers, maranta plant, magnifying glasses, umbrella.

What to do
Children's awareness of spring can be heightened by developing an interest in buds on plants. Let the children look closely at buds through a magnifying glass and draw their attention to the overlapping layers.

Show them a furled umbrella and point out the similarities.

Ask them what is needed to unfurl the buds. Can the children tell which of two twigs, or flowers, is the younger by looking at how open the buds, or petals, are? Older children may be able to put three twigs or flowers in order of age.

Bring in a maranta plant, which dramatically closes up when cold and opens in the warmth.

Look! I've made purple!

What you need
Powder paints, water, brushes, washing-up liquid bottles, coloured gummed labels, deep margarine pots and lids, scissors, mixing palettes.

What to do
Discovering the joys of mixing one's own colours is an exciting milestone in a child's aesthetic development. Let the children experiment with very small amounts of white and black paint added to other colours to create light and dark shades.

Most teachers will be familiar with the problem of paints turning into a uniform greyish brown sludge colour within a matter of moments! A way to avoid this is to fill washing-up liquid bottles with paint. Stick a colour-coded gummed label on each, and let the children squeeze a few drops from the bottles of their choice into a mixing palette.

Provide each child with a brush and a margarine tub (preferably the deep variety) filled with water, with a hole in the lid for the brush to go through. Encourage the children to swish their brushes around in the 'cleaning tubs' after each mixing operation, thus avoiding re-using dirty brushes.

Shades of autumn

What you need
Autumn leaves, bananas, melons etc.

What to do
Autumn leaves offer the young child enormous scope for sensory exploration. Take the children out on an autumn day to a place where leaves may be found in abundance. Encourage them to dance and twirl like the leaves.

Look closely at the different shades of green, brown, orange and yellow. Ask the children to arrange the leaves in order of age, basing their judgements on colour and texture. Bring in examples of fruit which is underripe, ripe and overripe (eg a hard green banana, a firm yellow banana and a soft brown banana). Ask the children to put them in order of ripeness.

Touch the ground

What you need
Any of the following, depending on availability: clay, mud, peat, grass, hay, straw, pebbles, gravel, wood shavings, sawdust, tea-leaves, sugar, salt.

What to do
To provide fully for a child's sensory exploration of the world, try to supplement the provision of sand and water with other natural resources, mentioning their origins. If you are using grass, hay or straw, watch out for children with allergies.

Take the children for a walk around the nursery or school to see how the ground forms a patchwork with all its different coverings, natural and man-made, such as grass, soil, gravel, pavement, tarmac. Talk about what is underneath the grass, pavement etc. Look out for weeds growing through cracks in the pavement. If possible, dig up a small square of turf for children to examine.

Living colour

What you need
Paint shade charts, limes, lemons, peaches, oranges, violets, copper bracelet, charcoal, stem ginger, honey etc; paints, brushes.

What to do
Provide children with the opportunity to look at, handle, smell and taste, where appropriate, the 'real thing' in relation to shades of colour of which they may only have heard the name.

Make 'living colour' displays, matching the colours on paint charts to their original namesakes from the natural world. Examples are oranges, tangerines, lemons, limes, peaches, violets, 'pinks' (carnations), marigolds, copper, ginger, honey and charcoal.

Children may enjoy trying to mix some of the colours and shades using paints.

It's magnetic

What you need
Magnets, magnetic and non-magnetic objects, magnetic letters, decorative refrigerator magnets, self-adhesive magnetic tape, metal trays, white paper, Blu-Tack, used greetings cards, scissors.

What to do
Older children will enjoy creating their own 'magnetic pictures'. Cut a piece of paper to cover a metal tray. Fix the paper in position with Blu-Tack. Give each child a metal tray covered with paper and a set of decorative refrigerator magnets. Ask the children to place a decorative magnet on the paper, and draw in an appropriate background for it.

Alternatively, let the children cut out animals, toys etc from used cards, and stick adhesive magnetic tape on to the back. The cut-outs can then be manoeuvred around on the tray by the child.

Funny bones

What you need
Pictures and models of skeletons, X-ray plates, two old umbrellas, child's plastic tent or playhouse, Mobilo or Asmeca, men's white handkerchieves or pieces of white sheet, pipe cleaners, pink Plasticine.

What to do
Some children believe that skeletons are rather scary, ghost-like creatures and have no understanding that we all have a skeleton inside our bodies. Help children understand that the skeleton is an internal supporting framework by letting them feel their own and each other's bones. Try to obtain X-ray plates, preferably of a child who has been to hospital. Bring in two old umbrellas. Remove the ribs of one umbrella and show the children how floppy it is without them. Remove the cover from another umbrella to expose the entire rib cage, and liken it to a skeleton.

Borrow a child's plastic play tent or playhouse, and show the child the frame without the cover. Let the children make miniature tents on the table with Play people, using Mobilo or Asmeca as 'frames', and covering them with men's white handkerchieves or pieces of white sheet.

Older children could make a simple body shape from pipe cleaners (the skeleton), with pink Plasticine wrapped around them for the skin.

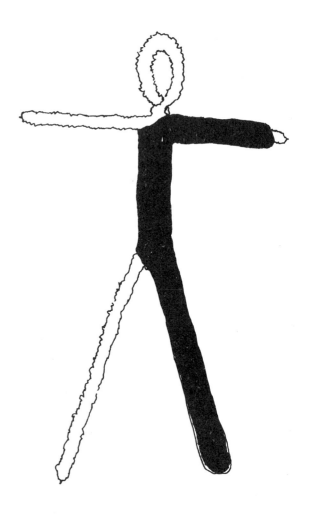

What's going on?

Chapter six

A child can begin to step outside her own immediate world once she begins to understand and use the various forms of communication that are now readily available. She can start to think beyond the present and consider people who are not immediately visible. She can be reminded about the past, for example, by looking at photographs, and be helped to think about future plans by having adults show her calendars and diaries.

Tickets please!

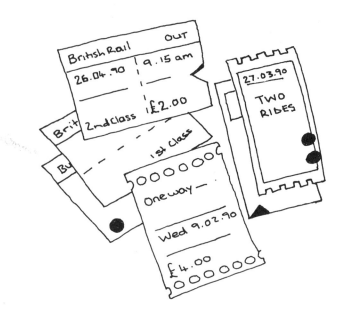

What you need
Used tickets of all kinds.

What to do
Send a letter home asking for the children to bring in used tickets. Make an attractive ticket display, which will lead to talk about time, place, numbers, money, destinations and past visits. 'Ticket offices' could be set up, and children could participate in a very simple raffle. (See also 'On the right track', page 34.)

It looks like rain

What you need
Sugar paper, scissors, card, felt-tipped pens, Velcro dots, or Blu-Tack.

What to do
Re-create a televised weather forecast. Let individual children take turns to be a weather presenter. Encourage them to predict the weather for the day by looking at the sky, and announce their prediction to the others. Instead of using a map, make a very simple wall weather-chart, using a bold outline drawing of the school building and grounds. Make symbols for cloud, sun, rain and wind from card, with Velcro dots or Blu-Tack on the back, which the children can stick on to their pictures.

In the news

What you need
Children's photographs, newspaper cuttings, adhesive, card, clear self-adhesive film, black felt-tipped pen.

What to do
There are many ways of interesting children in newspapers. For example, ask the children to bring in a clear photograph of themselves doing something interesting, either alone or with others. Photocopy each photograph and stick it on a piece of card. Chat with the child about what is happening in the picture, and let her dictate a short description. Write the description underneath the picture and, at the top of the card, put 'Please read to me' or 'Please read with me, using shared reading' (whichever is appropriate to your children). Cover each card with transparent film and let the children take home their own card, then later swap and take home each other's.

Another idea is to ask parents to send in interesting 'snippets' from local newspapers, sometimes about the children themselves.

Alternatively, find newspaper pictures which will appeal to young children (eg pets up to mischief) and stick them on to card. Write a simple description of what is happening underneath each picture. Cover these 'news cards' with film, and let the children take them home.

Look at my book

What you need
Children's books from home.

What to do
The pleasure children feel when their own book is read out at school is well known. Related fantasy and role play or a music and movement session is often carried out after the reading. As an alternative, plan to read a particular child's book and initiate a related fantasy or role play, or a music and movement session before reading the book (eg a session in the morning, with the related story being read in the afternoon). This can help introduce feelings of empathy for book characters. For example, if children have been role playing in the 'hospital' during the morning, and then a story about a child patient is read in the afternoon, the children can make a direct connection and begin to feel 'I'm like the child in the book'.

Exhibitions of books brought from home encourage discussion and comparisons and strengthen home-school links. Send home notes asking children to bring in books on different themes, just for one day, eg books about teddy bears, or other animals, favourite books, 'alphabet' books etc.

I went to the library

What you need
Contact with a children's librarian at a local library, card, narrow after-dinner mint chocolate box, date stamp, books to make a 'lending library'; dolls and cuddly toys.

What to do
Arrange to take the children to visit a nearby library and/or invite the children's librarian in to the classroom to talk to the children, and to 'act out' her role. Ask for one or two volunteers to pretend to return and borrow books. Ask the librarian to talk to them as she would in real life. Roles could then be reversed, and a child becomes the 'librarian'.

After the librarian's visit, set up a 'lending library' with as many authentic touches as possible, for example, librarian's counter, date stamp etc. Select a number of books for the 'library', and make simple 'cards' for them, which the 'librarian' can keep in a narrow after-dinner mint box. Take turns to play the roles of librarian and borrowers.

Follow-up
Extend the idea by encouraging the children to act out the role of a parent reading to a child.

Can you hear me?

What you need
Real or toy telephones, old radio, personal stereo, junk materials, black sticky paper, white gummed squares, felt-tipped pen, coiled kettle flex.

What to do
To help children explore the idea of talking with someone over a distance, devise structured play opportunities using telephones, radios etc. A new variant on the telephone theme is the car phone. Let the children make their own by covering a large toothpaste box with black sticky paper and sticking on small white gummed squares with numbers written on in felt-tipped pen. Children could act out the role of a doctor driving along 'on call', responding to an emergency.

Alternatively, tell the children about radio phones used by ambulance men and taxi drivers. A play variety can be made easily by using a plastic-coated coiled kettle flex attached to a small box (the microphone). The other end of the flex can be fitted to the 'dashboard' of the ambulance or taxi. Arrange for a taxi driver or an ambulance driver to bring their vehicles to school for the children to inspect.

What's on tonight?

What you need
Old television magazines, paper, paints, felt-tipped pens, letter to parents.

What to do
Television is a part of daily life for the vast majority of children and should be used to creative advantage to stimulate fantasy and role play as well as thinking and communication skills. Young children enjoy talking about their favourite programmes and show a keen interest in knowing on which day of the week they are shown. Build on this interest by bringing in old copies of television guides and pointing out the names of popular programmes, the days on which they occur, and the times. Send home a letter asking parents to go through a television magazine with their child and decide on a favourite programme. The parent could fill in a tear-off slip: '. . . likes to watch . . . on . . . at . . . o'clock'. Discuss this information with the children. Make a simple chart or book about favourite programmes, or a wall display, using children's paintings of programmes, completing sentences such as 'On Monday we like to watch . . .'

Let's choose a video

What you need
Video recorder, empty chocolate boxes with tops, roughly the size of a video cassette, paper, adhesive, felt-tipped pens, items for a 'video shop', eg a counter and simple shelving, shallow cardboard box such as that used for tomatoes, card, small white sticky labels.

What to do
Capitalise on children's interest in watching video films. Many parents are now buying or renting videos which are specially produced for children. Encourage the children to talk about the videos they enjoy, in the same way as you would books. Ask them to give the title, and say what happens and which characters they like best.

If a child brings a video to school, play a short excerpt to stimulate conversation and dramatic play.

Make a 'video shop', using empty chocolate boxes for the cassettes. Ask each child to draw a picture of a favourite film on a piece of paper the same size as the chocolate-box top. Help the child write the title, and stick the paper on to the box. Let the children act out the roles of the customer who asks for a particular film and the shopkeeper who has to find it. The customer could also ask the shopkeeper to talk about a certain film she has not seen but is thinking of borrowing.

Once they have returned from the shop, the children will want to 'watch' their 'video'. Discuss with them how to make a video player, perhaps using a shallow cardboard tomato box, with card for the top, a slot for the cassette to enter, and sticky labels for 'digital display'.

I'll just look it up on the computer

What you need
Cardboard boxes, greaseproof paper, adhesive, small white gummed squares, black felt-tipped pen.

What to do
Although your nursery or reception class may have access to a real computer, it is a good idea to give the children the chance to 'use' a mock computer in their fantasy and role play to help them come to see the computer as part of daily life.

Ask the children what they think could be used from the modelling area to make their own computer for everyone to share. A cardboard box with a square of greaseproof paper stuck on one side could be used as the screen, while small white labels stuck on a second, flatter box could represent the keyboard.

Talk about when and where they have seen computers being used, and why — by some parents in the home or at work, by the school secretary, in a shop or bank, or even in a 'space ship' on television. All of these ideas could stimulate structured play incorporating 'using' a computer. For example, talk about how a computer can help people find things out because it has a built-in memory.

Puppet show

What you need
Large plastic bottles, paper, pieces of
fabric, jewellery, wood, PVA adhesive,
thick pipe cleaners, card, felt-tipped pens.

What to do
The therapeutic value of puppets is
widely recognised. They have immediate
impact and are easy to use.

Children greatly enjoy making and
using puppets to create their own
versions of stories from books, television
or films.

Large plastic bottles covered in fabric
scraps and paper make bold and
effective puppets for very young children.
Pipe cleaners can be used to make arms,
and card decorated with felt-tipped pens
can be used for faces.

Reception children can plan the
puppets' dialogue.

I've got that comic

What you need
Used pre-school comics, card, clear self-adhesive film.

What to do
Many parents buy comics for their children. Ask the children to bring in old copies and use them in the following ways:

- Sort them into piles for a 'paper shop'.
- Cut off the titles and stick them on to card, then cover with film. Make two cards for each comic for children to play 'snap'.
- Choose a very simple picture story. Mount it on to card, cover it with clear self-adhesive film, and cut up the pictures. Let individual children put the pictures in sequence, then ask them to re-tell the story.

Alternatively, give the pictures to a pair of children to discuss together. Encourage co-operation by asking them to put them in the right sequence.

Looking forward

What you need
Shopping lists, assortment of telephone message pads, calendars and diaries belonging to staff members, sugar paper, hole punch, ribbon or string.

What to do
Help children to see how adults organise themselves by writing down future dates and plans.

Let the children watch you write out a shopping list.

Show them calendars, diaries and telephone message pads. Make a giant diary and hang it on the wall.

Let the children see you writing down reminders about what is going to happen on various days during the week or at different times of the day.

Letters

What you need
Items for letter writing such as stationery and 'stamps', letter box.

What to do
Letter writing is a motivating and realistic way of helping children develop concepts about written communication. Provide realistic items to encourage developmental writing: letters, shopping lists, phone messages, receptionists' notes, tickets, forms etc.

Devise imaginative contexts for sending and receiving letters. For example, Superted, who has had to go to the moon for a few days to sort out important business, is feeling a little lonely. Letters from the children (to whom, of course, he will reply!) would cheer him up enormously. His replies could be written on large sheets of paper, for reading with groups. Do not correct the children's invented spellings. (See also 'Look at my postcard', page 53.)

I know that song

What you need
Children's own song cassettes, paper or strong card, felt-tipped pens, clear acetate film, cassette recorder and headphones or earphones.

What to do
Children often bring in their favourite song cassettes. Write out the words of a child's favourite song, letting him listen to the cassette while you point to each word. Extend this idea by using the shared reading approach in a song context. Children love to see the words of their favourite songs written down. As they often half-know the words before they begin, with the rhyme, rhythm and repetition helping them to 'read' or sing the words straight away, the children invariably find they can 'read' the words instantly, which allows them to experience tremendous success. Write out the words of favourite songs on stiff card, decorate them with pictures, then cover them with clear acetate film. Let the children take these 'song cards' home for reading and singing together with their families.

Sometimes, a child may know a song that is unknown to you. She will be thrilled if you write down 'her' song on a song card for everyone to share. It may be necessary to ask the child's parents for the correct version of the song, as children often give a garbled version.

What are they learning?

Conclusion

To find out whether children are learning successfully, teachers must constantly ask themselves the question, 'What are they learning?' At the heart of the assessment process lies careful observation of the children's behaviour. The ideas given below are confined to practical suggestions for classroom observation, which is seen to be the teacher's most important tool for the promotion of successful learning. Although they conclude this book, they can also, of course, serve as a starting-point for teachers to make other kinds of assessments, both evaluative, in deciding possible next stages in learning, and summative, in 'summing up' a child's learning in relation to agreed norms.

A good starting-point is to realise that teachers are not the only observers of children, and to welcome and use parents' observations. Similarly, reception teachers can gain a valuable insight into children's potential by referring to the observations made by nursery staff, in pre-school records, as well as meeting with parents before a child starts school. Additionally, it can be beneficial for pre-school teachers and reception teachers to meet, preferably with parents too.

Children should be involved in the observation process. Reception children should be given the opportunity to say what they enjoy and dislike about school, what they think they are doing well in, and what they would like to improve. These comments by the children should be recorded by the teacher in the form of anecdotal records.

Anecdotal records of what children actually say and do can be very useful, provided organisational and practical concerns are accommodated. Many pre-school teachers have become good at observing what children say and do, and at recording their observations, and have a great deal of valuable expertise to share with reception teachers. For example, some pre-school teachers, working with a small group of children, write down what a child says he wants to do as he comes in, the first 'plan' of the day, and then add a few notes throughout the day about how the plan develops.

Records of this kind provide detailed information on individual children's interests and learning styles, which form the basis of informed discussion with parents, at parents' evenings etc.

Notes on recurrent 'schemas' observed, sayings by the child, interactions with other children, samples of drawings, paintings and models all help to contribute to a full, detailed picture of the child.

It can be very helpful to reception teachers, when teaching five-year-olds, to think of the National Curriculum statements of attainment as observations

of what children say and do in a wide variety of social and learning contexts. These should include informal settings with other children, as well as teacher-led situations. Certainly, children's learning in the National Curriculum cannot be left to chance, and must be carefully planned for by observing children's interests, so that these can be used as initial starting points to ensure motivation. For example, careful observation of what just three children are actually saying and doing in a day, can reveal a wealth of information showing that they are achieving a wide range of attainments. Teachers should look for the positive elements, for what children are doing in their interactions with others and in practical activities.

It is a good idea to note down not just what a child says and does (eg a statement of attainment), but also other factors involved such as the context, the circumstances and other children involved. This can give teachers ideas for possible areas of development.

There are many practical ways of managing and recording this continuing observation of children. For example:
• Make a class 'observation file', with dividers for different learning areas. 'Observation sheets' could be made in grid form, detailing the names of a group of children, statements of attainment (probably sub-divided) and the 'learning context' (topic, other children involved, date). As it is very difficult to write while interacting with the children, have a 'memory jogger' in the front of your file. Slip a list of all children's names into a plastic wallet and simply indicate with a

dot or coded letter those children you wish to write about at the earliest opportunity.

• In each 'interest area' of the room, hang up an exercise book, perhaps alphabetically indexed. As you notice anything interesting about a child's activities, jot down details, with the date of each activity.

• Use sticky gummed labels, carbon paper and alphabetical index boxes as additional aids to quick recording.

• Individual file folders, or a zig-zag alphabetical folder can be used to hold samples of drawings and paintings, children's drawings of models and writing, to build up a 'profile' of each child, for discussion at parents' evenings.

• Audio cassettes can be used a few times a year to record children reading aloud. Consider the use of video to record group interactions.

All of the above ideas can help to enable the teacher to achieve continuing, formative observations which record how children's learning develops.

Knickerbocker fun, see page 14

Other Scholastic books

Bright Ideas

The Bright Ideas books provide a wealth of resources for busy primary school teachers. There are now more than 20 titles published, providing clearly explained and illustrated ideas on topics ranging from *Word Games* and *Science* to *Display* and *Classroom Management*. Each book contains material which can be photocopied for use in the classroom.

Teacher Handbooks

The Teacher Handbooks give an overview of the latest research in primary education, and show how it can be put into practice in the classroom. Covering all the core areas of the curriculum, the *Teacher Handbooks* are indispensable to the new teacher as a source of information and useful to the experienced teacher as a quick reference guide.

Management Books

The Management Books are designed to help teachers to organise their time, classroom and teaching more efficiently. The books deal with topical issues, such as *Parents and Schools* and organising and planning *Project Teaching*, and are written by authors with lots of practical advice and experiences to share.

Let's Investigate

Let's Investigate is an exciting range of photocopiable activity books giving open-ended investigative tasks. Designed to cover the 6 to 12-year-old age range these books are ideal for small group or individual work. Each book presents progressively more difficult concepts and many of the activities can be adopted for use throughout the primary school. Detailed teacher's notes outlining the objectives of each photocopiable sheet and suggesting follow-up activities have been included.